21st Century Skills INNOVATION Library

Photography

by Annie Buckley

INNOVATION IN ENTERTAINMENT

Published in the United States of America by Cherry Lake Publishing
Ann Arbor, Michigan
www.cherrylakepublishing.com

Content Adviser: Tom Dowd, Columbia College Chicago

Design: The Design Lab

Photo Credits: Cover and page 3, paulaphoto, used under license from Shutterstock, Inc.; page 4, ©Dino Ablakovic, used under license from Shutterstock, Inc.; page 6, ©Scott Russo/ Wonderstock/Alamy; page 9, ©iStockphoto.com/proxyminder; page 11, Joseph Becker/Alamy; page 12, ©iStockphoto.com/stphillips; page 15, ©AP Photo/David Duprey; page 17, ©AP Photo; page 19, ©David Fleetham/Alamy; page 21, ©iofoto, used under license from Shutterstock, Inc.; page 22, ©Visual Arts Library (London)/Alamy; page 25, ©Tetra Images/Alamy; page 27, ©AP Photo/USPS; page 28, ©AP Photo/Dorothea Lange

Library of Congress Cataloging-in-Publication Data
Buckley, Annie.
 Photography / by Annie Buckley.
   p. cm.–(Innovation in entertainment)
 ISBN-13: 978-1-60279-221-0
 ISBN-10: 1-60279-221-6
 1. Photography–Juvenile literature. 2. Photography–History–Juvenile
literature. I. Title. II. Series.
 TR149.B764 2009
 770.9–dc22   2008002032

Cherry Lake Publishing would like to acknowledge the work of
The Partnership for 21st Century Skills.
Please visit www.21stcenturyskills.org for more information.

CONTENTS

Chapter One
The Early Days 4

Chapter Two
Tools of the Trade 9

Chapter Three
Creative Camera Work 16

Chapter Four
The Business of Photography 20

Chapter Five
Innovators in Photography 26

Glossary 30
For More Information 31
Index 32
About the Author 32

The Early Days

Camera phones are a convenient way to take photos on the go.

"Smile, Grandpa!" Emily snapped a photo with her digital camera. Then she looked at the image and said, "Oh, it came out great! See?"

Her grandfather looked at the display on the back of the camera and shook his head. "Amazing. When I was your age, we developed film in a **darkroom**. Now you just print photos from your computer."

"What are darkrooms?" Emily asked.

The older man chuckled, then started to tell her all about them.

✳ ✳ ✳

Today, photographs are everywhere. They are blown up to billboard size or shrunk to fit inside a wallet. Photography began as a complicated and time-consuming process. But now, capturing an image is as fast and easy as pushing a button on a cell phone. The history of photography goes back less than 200 years. But it's a rich history and one that is still **evolving**.

In the fifth century BCE, a Chinese philosopher named Mo-tzu noticed something important. He saw that if light enters a small hole, it can project an upside-down image on an opposite wall. Centuries later, some artists used a method called the pinhole process to help them draw more realistically. They projected images onto paper or canvas with a box called a camera obscura. But to capture the image on paper or canvas, they had to trace or sketch it. That's because as soon as the light was removed, these images disappeared.

The camera obscura wasn't anything like the cameras we know today. But it helped spark the imagination of artists, scientists, and inventors in many parts of the world. They wondered if it was possible to create a device that could permanently capture realistic images.

Joseph Niépce of France is an important figure in photography's history. Niépce was interested in a type

This daguerreotype of firefighters in Charleston, South Carolina, dates to the 1850s.

of printing called **lithography**. Eventually, he turned his attention to finding a way to make pictures with a camera obscura. On a window, he set up a camera with a lens, hoping to capture the view. He projected the image onto a metal plate that had been prepared with special chemicals. Those chemicals reacted with the projected light. This allowed light to create an image on the plate. This image is the first permanent photograph from nature. The year was 1826.

A theater artist named Louis Daguerre also wanted to make a lasting image with a camera. Daguerre heard of Niépce's research. The two men shared ideas and discoveries for about four years until Niépce died. In 1837, their combined efforts helped lead to Daguerre's creation of the first practical process of making lasting images with a camera. He called the resulting pictures daguerreotypes. They were made on metal plates and placed under glass for display. Before long, daguerreotypes became wildly popular. Daguerreotypes, however, could not be reproduced. They were one of a kind.

About the same time, an English scientist was exploring a different method of making images with the camera. William Henry Fox Talbot invented a two-step photographic process using a **negative** to print an image. The images created from this process were called calotypes. With this method, multiple copies of an image could be made. At first, this method was not as popular as daguerreotypes. The process was still fragile and expensive. But over time, it became the preferred way of making photographs. Today, photographs made

In 1829, Daguerre and Niépce formed a partnership. They combined their efforts and worked together to improve the technology of photography. They did experiments on their own, but shared their knowledge by communicating their ideas in coded letters. Daguerre and Niépce understood that they could benefit and learn from each other's experiences. This collaboration helped lead to the invention of the daguerreotype.

Do you think it is important for scientists to share their findings and research with each other?

with traditional film still use a two-step process.

Digital cameras are part of the newest stage in photography's evolution. They first became available to the public in the 1990s. It may be just a matter of time before traditional film photography becomes a thing of the past. Along with digital cameras, the photo-editing software and photo printers available today help make photography more popular and accessible than ever.

Tools of the Trade

Through the years, camera technology has been updated and improved. But the basic concept behind the modern camera is similar to the camera obscura. A camera consists of a box, or camera body. A hole, called an aperture, is covered by a glass lens. When you take a picture, a tiny door in the camera called the shutter opens. This allows light to hit a sensitized film or plate to make an image. Photographers can adjust the size of the aperture and the length of time the shutter stays open. This controls how much light passes through the lens.

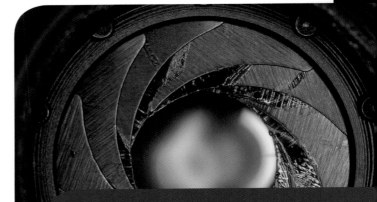

The size of the aperture partly determines which objects in a photograph will be in focus.

Innovations in cameras and lenses have made them lighter and easier to use. In the past, photographers would have to take great care to get the focus and other aspects of the shot just right. The film they used required the camera's shutter to be open for minutes at a time just to get enough light for a usable image. Today's automatic cameras set the aperture and shutter speed for you. These improvements helped create a much larger market for cameras. They allowed almost anyone to take pictures. Because the camera adjusts itself, chances are you'll end up with a decent photograph. Still, being aware of the amount of light and other technical aspects of photography is very important. It can make the difference between an okay photograph and a great one. That is why most professional photographers still adjust camera settings themselves.

The chemistry involved in photography has undergone many changes. In the early days, the metal plates and paper negatives used in photography were very fragile. This often made it difficult to reproduce, store, or transport the recorded images. An important innovation came in 1851. An English sculptor and photographer named Frederick Scott Archer discovered how to make glass negatives. His wet collodion process produced images that not only were clear, but could be

It can be difficult to recognize an image on negative film because the tones are reversed.

reproduced consistently. This development was a step toward the negative film still in use today.

To produce a photograph with a film camera, an image is first recorded onto negative film. Its tones appear to reverse—light is dark and dark is light. The negative is then processed with chemicals. This fixes the image so that it cannot accidentally be damaged by more light. The resulting negative is printed on light-sensitive paper in a specialized place called a darkroom. An **enlarger** projects the negative onto photographic paper. Then the paper is passed through chemical baths until the image appears on the paper. When the image appears on the photographic paper, the tones are reversed again. Dark becomes dark and light becomes light to match the original image.

Early photographs needed a lot of light to create a usable image. If the photographer used only the available sunlight, it could take minutes or even hours to create the image. Photographers realized they could get more light by blowing magnesium powder into a low flame. This produced a flash of bright white light just as the picture was taken. But this method was messy and very dangerous.

In 1930, smokeless flashbulbs became available in the United States. But they could be used only once.

In the darkroom, photographers use tongs to handle photographs. This protects their hands from the chemicals used to develop photos.

Inventors solved this problem by creating cameras with built-in flash devices. Today's modern electronic flash devices can be used over and over. They often have sensors that automatically adjust the flash settings to create just the right amount of light needed.

For many decades, photographs were available only in black and white. Artists and inventors explored ways to make color photographs. Some painted directly on the black-and-white prints. Then in 1942, Eastman Kodak introduced color film under the brand name Kodacolor.

Another exciting development came in 1948 when Polaroid introduced the first instant camera. Instant cameras produced a finished print within minutes. In the early 2000s, cell phones with cameras became the preferred method of taking "instant" pictures.

Learning & Innovation Skills

In 1993, an inventor named Daniel A. Henderson developed **prototypes** for a wireless picturephone. It would receive images and video data. Soon after, several companies were trying to find a practical way to put a camera in a cell phone. In 1997, Philippe Kahn put together a rough model of a camera phone. Kahn is credited as the cell phone camera's inventor. It didn't take long for the idea to catch on. In 2006, companies sold 460 million cell phones with cameras.

By acting on a creative idea, Kahn helped introduce the world to a new form of technology. In what ways do you think camera phones have changed how we share images?

After years of relying on film, inventors began to ask: What if there were a camera that didn't use film at all? In 1975, an engineer for Kodak named Steven Sasson created a device that changed the world of photography. It was about the size of a toaster and weighed 8 pounds (3.6 kilograms). This awkward device was a rough model of the digital camera. In 1981, Sony marketed the first filmless camera. It was called the Mavica and was based on television technology. It wasn't technically a digital camera. Still, the camera industry was starting to move in a different direction, away from film. But the digital camera didn't catch on with buyers or even manufacturers for years.

Digital cameras capture images on a light-sensitive chip, or sensor. The sensor records each image as a digital file. Digital pictures can be downloaded from the camera to the computer. Manufacturers realized that people really like being able to see their photos right away. And because the images were saved as digital files, they could be e-mailed or printed directly from the camera's memory card with ink-jet printers. Digital images, unlike negatives, can be stored in a computer database. They can then be edited using software. This software allows people to change **contrast** or retouch images.

In the late 1990s, the popularity of digital cameras exploded. By 2005, half of American households had a

Through the years, the digital camera has evolved from a large, bulky device into smaller, more compact models.

digital camera. And that percentage continues to increase. The many benefits of digital cameras have helped make photography a hobby for many people.

CHAPTER THREE

Creative Camera Work

Soon after the invention of the camera, people began playing with different ways to shoot images. In the 1800s, a style called high art photography emerged. High art photographers carefully arranged the people or objects in their photos. Their photos often told some kind of story or stirred up an emotion. Sometimes, the images drew inspiration from literature, paintings, or history. Henry Peach Robinson combined many individual photographs into one to make **composite** images.

Later in the century, a style of art called modernism influenced photographers such as Edward Weston and Paul Strand. Photographers at this time were not interested in making pictures based on paintings. They used the camera to make a new kind of art. They took pictures of everyday objects such as fruits and vegetables. They

Ansel Adams loved to photograph nature and worked to protect the environment. He's shown here with *Monolith: The Face of Half Dome, 1927*, a view of Yosemite National Park.

took advantage of the camera's special way of capturing light and shadow. The photographer Ansel Adams used these ideas to make unique photographs of landscapes. This was an important moment in photography's history.

Learning & Innovation Skills

Some of the most creative ideas in cameras come from the world of espionage. Spy gadgets don't just exist in the movies. For years, they've been used in real life to obtain top-secret information. In the late 1930s, Walter Zapp invented the Minox camera. It took clear pictures and was small enough to hide inside a fist. The camera was used to secretly photograph important documents, places, and people. Today, spy cameras can be hidden in surprising places like watches.

Spies are on a mission. Using special tools like tiny cameras, they must be able to analyze and make sense of complex or unorganized information. In what ways do you think cameras help spies solve problems and find answers?

Photography was establishing itself as a unique art form.

Other innovations in photography have helped science and research. Scientists use microscopes with cameras to photograph cells and organisms. Special cameras and equipment can take pictures underwater, in outer space, or in complete darkness. Astronauts using special cameras took the first photographs of Earth from the moon in 1968. Today, NASA places cameras on satellites and deep space probes to take pictures of the farthest reaches of our solar system.

Photography also plays an important role in the news. In photojournalism, photographers take pictures to document people and events around the world. Photojournalists have to be creative and flexible. They use fast, lightweight cameras and accurate lenses to record important moments in history. With digital cameras, modern photojournalists can take pictures that can be available within moments for viewing or printing almost anywhere in the world.

Can you think of some challenges that underwater photographers face?

CHAPTER FOUR

The Business of Photography

One of the most popular uses of photography is **portraiture**. Before daguerreotypes, portraits were painted by hand on canvas. Only wealthy people could afford them. Photography made it possible for regular folks to have their portraits made. In the 1800s, photographic studios sprang up all over Europe and the United States. This was the start of the business of photography.

In the early days, some photographers created portable businesses to market their services. They packed everything they needed into a tent or wagon and traveled from town to town taking portraits. Today's portrait photographers advertise their services for all sorts of pictures. These include **headshots** for actors. Other portrait photographers take pictures at weddings or other important events.

Photographers set up studios to take images of models, as well as families and children.

One of the biggest changes in the photography business came in 1888 when George Eastman introduced his first camera. He invented a way for people to take pictures and send the film to his company to be processed. He knew that most people would buy only one camera. But if he processed their film, they would keep coming back for more film and processing. That means

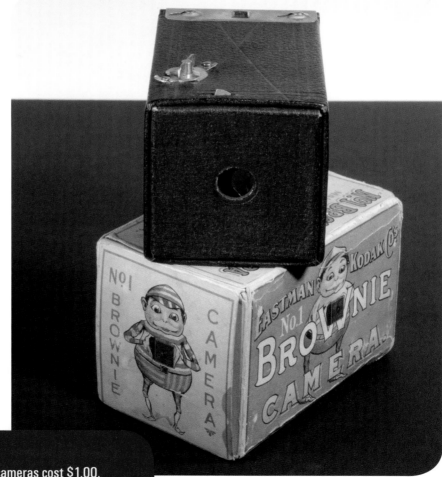

The first Kodak Brownie cameras cost $1.00.

he would keep making money. He called his company Eastman Kodak, named for himself and the simple early camera the company produced.

In 1900, Kodak changed photography with the Brownie. It was a small, box-shaped camera that took 100 pictures on a single roll of film. People didn't have to understand chemistry or buy expensive equipment to take photographs. They just had to point and shoot. Now anyone could take pictures.

Because photography uses technology that is always changing, companies must innovate and change to survive. One of the reasons Kodak continues to thrive is that the company knows it needs to stay competitive. It has kept up with technological innovations in photography. Rather than resist changes, Kodak tries to

Learning & Innovation Skills

 If companies want to stay in business, they need to keep up with the latest technological developments. In the 1940s, American inventor Edwin Land designed an instant camera. This camera had self-developing film that allowed people to see their images in minutes. They didn't have to send the film somewhere to be processed. Land's company, Polaroid, enjoyed many years of success with the instant camera. However, demand fell sharply by the start of the 21st century. Film in general was less popular. People were turning to digital cameras. By 2008, Polaroid announced plans to end production of instant film. Polaroid will now focus on and produce digital photography and television products.

Why do you think Polaroid decided to stop production of instant film? What do you think would happen to Polaroid if it didn't change its focus?

stay current. For example, Kodak saw the potential of digital photography. Since the 1980s, the company has been producing and developing image sensors for digital cameras. Those are the light-sensitive chips that help record images.

In the 1990s, digital cameras were made widely available to the public. Companies realized they could make a lot of money selling computer software and ink-jet printers for making and printing photos at home. Digital cameras and computer software made it possible for ordinary people to be creative with photographs. Two brothers named Thomas Knoll and John Knoll invented what became Adobe Photoshop in the 1980s. This computer program was released in 1990. It is still one of the most popular photo-imaging programs available. Selling digital cameras, computer software, and photo printers is big business. Companies work to make better and faster equipment all the time.

Where is the future of photography headed? Scientists are trying to find ways to make even clearer photos. The Foveon X3 direct image sensor is one innovation. This advanced sensor helps produce very sharp images with excellent color quality. If the X3 catches on, it could become the new standard in camera technology. The cameras of the future will also have more memory for storing photos and more options for creative

Most people who print photos at home don't use ordinary paper. They use special photo paper.

photo taking. Some scientists even imagine that we will be able to touch and smell three-dimensional images in the years to come. Whatever the future holds, one thing is certain: people will always want to take pictures and share them with one another.

Innovators in Photography

There have been many creative thinkers who have brought their ideas to the field of photography. Here are just a few of the innovators who have helped make photography an art form enjoyed by people around the world.

William Henry Fox Talbot

William Henry Fox Talbot was an English scientist and landowner. He invented a two-step photographic process. It used paper negatives to print reproducible photographic pictures. He called them calotypes. His work *Pencil of Nature* was the first commercially produced book that had photographs.

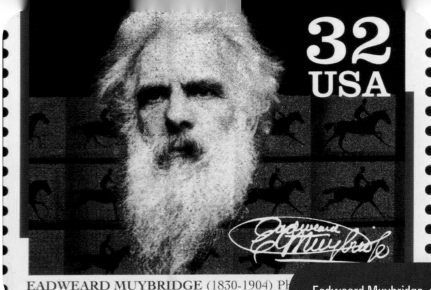

EADWEARD MUYBRIDGE (1830-1904) Ph[...]
1996

Eadweard Muybridge, shown here on a U.S. postage stamp, invented the zoopraxiscope, an ancestor of the modern film projector.

Eadweard Muybridge

Eadweard Muybridge was an English photographer who lived and worked in San Francisco in the late 1800s. Muybridge was a true innovator. He was one of the first photographers to experiment with motion. He took many pictures of one action, such as a horse running. In 1879, he invented the zoopraxiscope. This machine used multiple pictures of an action and re-created the motion. The pictures played together like a movie—before movies were invented!

Alfred Stieglitz

Alfred Stieglitz helped bring attention to photography as an art form. Stieglitz believed in using

21st Century Content

Dorothea Lange was an American photojournalist and documentary photographer. In the 1930s, the Great Depression was affecting the United States and much of the world. Many people lost their jobs and homes. People struggled just to get enough to eat. Lange helped capture this moment in history. She photographed people who were homeless. She was hired by the U.S. government to take photographs of farmers. Her emotional photographs of migrant families and children were published in newspapers and magazines. Her photographs raised awareness and helped bring much needed aid to these people.

Lange's efforts show the power of photographs to address global issues like poverty. Many times, pictures make stronger statements than words. What do you think you can learn about your culture and society by studying a photograph? What can you learn about other cultures from photos from different nations?

the camera as a tool, like a paintbrush. He believed that photographers should create images, not just follow directions for taking and printing pictures. He broke with many **conventions** of photography at the time. For example, he found ways to take photographs in the rain, snow, and at night, instead of waiting for the perfect lighting. He also showed that photographers could use creativity when they developed images in the darkroom. In 1902, Stieglitz helped establish an organization of photographers called the Photo-Secession, which organized photography shows. Beginning in 1903, he published a journal called *Camera Work*.

Many of Dorothea Lange's photos from the Great Depression focus on the emotions and expressions of people.

Glossary

collaboration (kuh-lab-uh-RAY-shuhn) the act of working together to get something done

composite (kuhm-PAHZ-it) made up of many different parts

contrast (KON-trast) the level of difference between the lightest and darkest areas of a photograph

conventions (kuhn-VEN-shuhnz) accepted ways of behaving or thinking

darkroom (DARK-room) a special room used for developing photos

documentary (dok-yu-MEN-tuh-ree) related to facts or information instead of an imaginary story

enlarger (en-LARJ-ur) a device that projects images from a negative onto photographic paper

espionage (ESS-pee-uh-nahzh) the act of spying or use of spies to get secret information

evolving (ih-VAHLV-eeng) developing over time through changes

headshots (HED-shotss) photographs of a person's head or face, often used by actors

lithography (lith-AH-gruh-fee) a printing process using ink and special plates

migrant (MY-gruhnt) describing a person who moves often from one place to another in search of work

negative (NEG-uh-tihv) an image on a special material in which dark areas are light and light areas are dark; negatives can be used to print photographs

portraiture (POR-tri-chur) the making of portraits

prototypes (PROH-tuh-tipess) original models of an invention

For More Information

BOOKS

Bidner, Jenni. *The Kids' Guide to Digital Photography: How to Shoot, Save, Play with & Print Your Digital Photos*. New York: Lark Books, 2004.

Litwin, Laura Baskes. *Dorothea Lange: A Life in Pictures*. Berkeley Heights, NJ: Enslow Publishers, 2008.

Richter, Joanne. *Inventing the Camera*. New York: Crabtree Publishing Company, 2006.

WEB SITES

Big Learning Photography for Kids
www.biglearning.com/treasure-photography-for-kids.htm
Links to photography information and project ideas for kids

Henry Ransom Center: The First Photograph
www.hrc.utexas.edu/exhibitions/permanent/wfp/
Learn more about Joseph Niépce's early experiments with photography

William Henry Fox Talbot
www.metmuseum.org/TOAH/HD/tlbt/hd_tlbt.htm
For more on one of photography's greatest innovators

Index

Adams, Ansel, 17
Adobe Photoshop software, 24
aperture, 9, 10
Archer, Frederick Scott, 10
art, 16–18, 27–28
astronauts, 18

body, 9
Brownie camera, 23

calotypes, 7, 26
camera obscura, 5–6, 7, 9
Camera Work journal, 28
cell phones, 5, 13
chemicals, 7, 11
collaboration, 7, 8
color, 13, 24
composite images, 16
computers. *See* software.
contrast, 14

Daguerre, Louis, 7, 8
daguerreotypes, 7, 8
darkrooms, 11, 28
digital photography, 8, 14–15, 19, 24

Eastman, George, 21–23
Eastman Kodak company, 13, 14, 23–24
enlargers, 11
equipment sales, 23–24
espionage, 18

film, 11, 22–23
flashbulbs, 12
flash devices, 12–13
focus, 10
Foveon X3 sensor, 24
future, 24–25

Great Depression, 28

headshots, 20
Henderson, Daniel A., 13
high art photography, 16

instant cameras, 13, 23

Kahn, Philippe, 13
Knoll, John, 24
Knoll, Thomas, 24
Kodacolor film, 13

Land, Edwin, 23
Lange, Dorothea, 28
lenses, 6, 9, 10, 18
light, 5, 7, 9, 10, 11, 12–13, 14, 17, 24, 28
lithography, 6

magnesium, 12
Mavica camera, 14
microscopes, 18
Minox camera, 18
modernism, 16–17
motion pictures, 26–27
Mo-tzu (Chinese philosopher), 5
Muybridge, Eadweard, 26–27

negatives, 7, 10–11
news, 18–19
Niépce, Joseph, 7, 8

photographic paper, 11–12
photojournalists, 18–19
Photo-Secession organization, 28
pinhole process, 5
Polaroid company, 13, 23

portraiture, 20
printers, 8, 14, 24
processing, 7, 8, 10–12, 22–23

Robinson, Henry Peach, 16

Sasson, Steven, 14
scientists, 18, 24, 25
sensors, 13, 14, 24
shutters, 9, 10
software, 8, 14, 24
space exploration, 18
spy cameras, 18
Stieglitz, Alfred, 27–28
Strand, Paul, 16

Talbot, William Henry Fox, 7, 26
two-step photographic process, 7, 8, 26

Weston, Edward, 16
wet collodion process, 10–11

Zapp, Walter, 18
zoopraxiscope, 26–27

About the Author

Annie Buckley is a writer, artist, and children's book author. She first studied photography in high school and has since experimented with printing photographs on different materials, such as fabric and metal. She now makes photo collages using digital photos and a computer. One of the things Annie likes best about photography is its ability to communicate both about the world around us and the world of the imagination.